Ash Dickinson is a poet, perfo[...]
He has become one of the l[...]
word performers since turning
A multiple slam champion, incl[...]
and BBC Radio, Ash has perforn[...]
Canada, USA, Spain, Jordan, the Czech Republic and Germany
and has headlined many shows and festivals throughout the
UK, and he is in great demand to run workshops. His debut
collection, *Slinky Espadrilles* (2012), was the first book published
by Burning Eye Books. His second collection, Strange Keys,
also released by Burning Eye, came out in 2016.
Ash often runs poetry workshops and gives talks: in education at
all levels, through art education (libraries, museums, prisons) and
with adult writing groups. He has been invited to showcase his
workshops at secondary school heads-of-English conferences
for Hertfordshire, Devon, Cheshire and Hull, and to the Rugby
Group. He has addressed the literary society at Stowe School
three times, and he was a case study in the Bloomsbury-
published classroom aid *Making Poetry Happen* (2015).

For JESSICA!
HAPPY READING!

SHOW CATS IN TRANSIT

Ash Dickinson

Bx3

This edition published by Bx3, an imprint of Burning Eye Books 2019

www.burningeye.co.uk

@burningeyebooks

Burning Eye Books
15 West Hill, Portishead, BS20 6LG

ISBN 978-1-911570-80-6

SHOW CATS
IN TRANSIT

CONTENTS

DINOSAURS

dinosaurs
died out because
of their design flaws

it wasn't the meteor
the meteor was just the final straw
the final thing   a dino   saw

THE BOY WHO ATE ONLY BUTTER

as a boy, I ate only butter
thick golden slices straight from the fridge
or spooned on unending summer evenings
as it pooled, left out, into winners' medals

some nights it was impossible to tell
where sun ended and butter began

despairing, my parents lashed it
on everything, but I steered a path around
wolfed it down before it melted in
I was a stubborn child
butter was all I craved

I was twelve
when Mum brought home something new –
I Can't Believe It's Not Butter
just try it, she said, sliding the tub towards me
we have to tighten our belts
with your dad's job uncertain
and TV insists it's the same

sceptically, I lifted the lid
inside was what looked like mince
a scoop of mash, some terrified peas
a small portion of sherry trifle
and two sticky and loose After Eight mints
and people mistook this for butter?!
I couldn't believe it!

my parents hovered like fireflies
hot-eyed and scarcely breathing
transfixed as I tentatively dipped
into that patchwork spread –
it was the oddest butter I'd ever tried…!

and yet the strangest thing was this –
every time we ran out a new tub would arrive
looking utterly different to the one that came before it!
at times it resembled ham
or bananas, hazelnuts, cream cheese
spaghetti, green beans
and just once, dizzyingly, profiteroles

I told Mum I thought
I Can't Believe It's Not Butter was magic
I'm not sure she understood
for whilst doing other things
she lightly ruffled my fringe
and said she thought I would

placing a new tub in front of me
her smile serene and buttery
she said it's likely this one
has undertones of fish cakes

STATUS UPDATE POEM

what's on your mind today?
tell your friends/ without delay
a status update/ are things ok?

Ash is performing in Leeds
Ash has lost his keys
Ash is out of cereal… again
Ash has had a wardrobe malfunction – one fell on him
Ash is wishing they'd remake some lame eighties TV show
Ash has turned into a giant otter

Friday: Ash has a new girl in his life and can't stop smiling
Saturday: Ash is seeing new girl again tonight – woohoo
(three exclamation marks/ smiley face emoji)
Sunday: Ash is dumped

Monday: Ash has just got up
Ash has brushed his teeth
Ash has gone to the loo
Ash has done a number two
Ash has washed his hands
Ash has made some toast –
a perfect collaboration of colour and crunch
though/ as you know/ Ash hates to boast
it's only five to eight/ Ash is already on his day's ninth update

Ash should probably go outside –
it looks sunny and his papery skin is crepe
Ash has way too much time on his hands
and ought to physically see some of these mates
Ash is finally having a thought
he doesn't feel the need/ to communicate

MANGO, THE READING RETRIEVER

Mango, the reading retriever
is read to by primary pupils
to improve literacy
it has worked
she is now the most well-read canine
in the country

with a reading age of twelve
(which in dog years is seventy-seven)
she laps up complex sentence structure –
to her, a book is worth any bone from any butcher
this precociousness
eventually led to her enrolment in class
in no time, she rose to be head girl

when she dreams, she dreams
of pea-green boats, fields of rabbits
sent scattering as she runs to sand
wet as her nose, to search the horizon
for Robinson Crusoe, go
where the wild things go, go
to meet the mouse that knows the Gruffalo

when she whimpers, front leg a-twitch
she has found lost treasure
that attracts four children
the whole world ahead of them
an endless summer opening up
like the unimaginable pleasure
that awaits you in a book

WHIPLASH

the first thing I noticed were her eyes
emboldened, magnified by mascara
so that practically a third
of her face
was eye

practically a third
of her face
was eye

and still she never noticed me

STAR WARS IN THREE MINUTES

a long time ago
in a galaxy far, far away
from CGI rethinks
and technically-after-
but-mercifully-before
Jar Jar Binks

a star destroyer
long, black and ominous
like Vader's cloak
Leia uploads a YouTube video
Obi-Wan, you're my only hope
stopping
she wonders if it'll get more hits
than the one of Jabba   body-popping
R2, 3PO in a pod for hours
land in sand, get separated
get jumped by jawas
bought by Uncle Owen and Aunt Beru
twin suns, a daydreaming nephew
cue wistful music and a bad transistor
cut to Luke getting the hots/ for his sister
R2 does a runner
so too the Tusken raiders
they'll be back   and in greater number
Ben shuffling on looking simply like a coat
(there's more of this to come, you know)
Luke, you must learn the ways of the force
I can't, I've got to get home or I'll be in big trouble
arrives home… *ah, my relatives are smouldering rubble*
ok, set a course

for Mos Eisley
a more wretched hive of scum and villainy
there isn't   outside of Leeds
greed is good, Greedo is not
Han takes him out with one low shot

15

that's right – Han Solo   and Chewbacca
Harrison Ford in the role that made him
and a seven-foot-tall English actor
dressed in carpet chic
hanging out in a bar
that looks like Dresscodes Nightclub in Mansfield
only with less freaks
he's got the Millennium Falcon
and is taking Luke, the old man and the droids to Alderaan
but grrr! it's just been pulverised by the Empire!
the sat nav says: *you've reached your destination*
but it's just rock fragments, obliterated Bantha Burger Kings
…and a massive space station
of course they try to flee the scene
but   *irony*, thinks Luke
you try to escape the farming industry
only to be caught in a tractor beam
then a trash compactor
and that only after
you've dressed up as a stormtrooper
and rescued a future queen
and just when things seem ok
Obi-Wan becomes a coat again
struck down by Vader's 'saber
the Sith Lord pokes it with a foot
picks it up, puts it in the recycling
it's found shortly by the Death Star's night porter
thinks *ooh, it's nice thick cloth*
will come in handy   *should there be a sequel*
on the ice planet Hoth

our heroes escape
though I should mention the fire-fight scrape
and the palpable romantic tension
oddly it's Han that repeatedly calls Leia 'sister'
and in real life he was old enough to father Carrie Fisher
but I digress
cut to hyperspace
a homing beacon tracking the rebel base

16

who counter-analyse plans to defeat them
and it's a countdown
I'll have a T, I, E
a Y, an X   and next
the rebel force are in the sky
scything along the Death Star's trench
getting shot up until it looks like Luke's by himself
the Empire getting way too close for the rebels' health
if only Han hadn't scuttled off when he did
hang on
...great shot, kid!
Luke's aimed a torpedo
Vader's spinning like disco
the Death Star lit up like a glitter ball
medals to all necks but the wookiee's
Han wondering if he can eBay his
one-nil to the rebels
cue John Williams
roll closing titles

HAIKU INTERLUDE I

gave you a shoulder
provided you with an ear
now I look quite odd

fun onion: funion
a new type of vegetable
makes you laugh, not cry

is it socks or gloves
that make a suitable gift
for an octopus?

SHADOW-BOXING SNOWFLAKES

blond youngster maybe eight
shadow-boxing snowflakes
each stands in the way
of his title hopes
pins one with a low jab
tight up against the shelter ropes
a second lands on his tongue
what's my name?! he taunts its tingle
a single swift and brutal swallow
another challenger slain, gone

come morning there will be a thick white canvas
commuters standing awed and helpless
but this first fall – so unannounced and small
makes the boy dance, entranced
flick a fast right deep, distributing weight
a line settling on his knuckles
cloaks where the punches scrape
towelling white collar working bomber nape

fall in all comers, float, fight
give out boxer, all your might
a combination, two left, one right
rock it, shock the snow
bring about a knockout blow
a muffled yet conclusive bell
a soft-shoe shuffle, the victory yell

confetti fell! ticker tape! the train
appears, nears, as it brakes
he hears the acclaim, the fame
the echoed chanting of his name
great wheels squeal steel applause

and the bigger it comes
the harder, still, it falls

FREE RANGE EGGS

what's the point of free-range eggs
they can't go anywhere
they don't have any legs

SHOWER GEL

my shower gel has written on it
in big letters, the words
'Peaceful and Soothing
Shower Gel'

this seems an odd boast
for a shower gel to make
certainly, though, it has never
given me a moment's trouble
if I look miserable when showering
it is tremendously comforting
saying things like c'mon, Ash
remember what an awesome life you lead
before emitting a little bubble
that makes me go all giddy
and giggle like a toddler

and peaceful?
never have you seen
such a placid temperament
it successfully intervened
in the shampoo/conditioner riots
of two-thousand-nine
it is the Kofi Annan of wash-time
this manner runs in the family, it says
its great-grandfather shower gel
refused the Vietnam draft
fleeing instead to Canada
to preach peace
and make Canadians clean
and tingly

recently, in a hurry, half-asleep
I picked up, by mistake, in a supermarket
a 'Malevolent and Antagonising
Shower Gel'

I now only take baths

ONE WEEK AT SEA

on a black afternoon
I went down to meet the Ocean
he shook me by the sand
and we swapped tales of desolation
until the sun dropped from the sky

after much sorrow
I suggested we exchange lives
I'd been in a bar all morning
but failed to see what either of us had to lose –
we were miserable
let's try it for a week, see how things go
then reconvene

after some thought he agreed –
rose up from the depths
as tall as the Adam's apple on the man in the moon
shook himself like a wet dog
free of coral and crustacean
and I lay down beside him
and opened my mouth wide enough
to swallow whales and rays and sea cucumbers
and fish as ugly as people in crowd scenes in films

when I was full of all the contents of the Ocean
I asked him what he was going to do now
I aim to find that bar and get tipsy, he replied
though, he said, I think I can hold my drink
and with a wink I watched him slink away
he shouted back something about me
having to go out in five minutes
and then he was gone

to put it mildly it was quite a lifestyle change
to have boats sail on my stomach
and the first time a man dived into my mouth
I think I may have gagged

and spat him out
I heard the diver remark that the sea was rough today
so I thought it best to mellow

my back felt stiff at intervals – lying down all day as I did
and every so often I would shift
this action, unfortunately
resulted in numerous capsizings and drownings
ships absorbed through my pores

being the sea carries a large responsibility, I quickly learnt
my insides took care of themselves
no change there
big fish ate little fish
and wrecked vessels
got tangled in veins and ventricles
held like octopus tentacles

every morning I would get up   and walk out a mile
                                        and lie down
and stay there until evening
at which point I would return to my original spot
I understood this was how Ocean got his exercise
I also discovered, perhaps for the first time in my life, real love
people needed me – embraced me with their surfboards
and their pedaloes, children laughing in my hair
dogs, in particular, loved me
but would frequently pee in me
as did children
and adults   when they thought no one was watching

after three days I found a crisp packet in my ear
and a Coke can and an old tyre and shoes
and I began to choke
waste was everywhere
I tried to cough but all that came up was plastic and tin
and I raged in a sickness –
threw captains from their perch
and to perch I gave headaches

my insides bubbling
and turtles and sealions would balance on my teeth
afraid to enter

this continued for four days –
four days of whirlpools and rips, giant swells
all the people disappeared
all the aquatic life put their fins together in prayer
until, at last, I saw Ocean approaching
over the peak of a mountain
it was good to see him

Ocean, I said, with barely disguised relief
are you ready to change back?
but I knew
I knew now, with all that I had experienced
that he would never trade
that I was stuck forever as the sea
and with this
I become more miserable than I ever thought possible

suddenly Ocean stretched and lay beside me
summoned marlin to jump from my throat and into him
and I emptied like a night on cheap wine –
all the dolphins, all the eels, all the seals

purged, I lay looking at the night stars
a great weight gone from me
felt the cool air on my face
why, Ocean? I asked. why return to this?

for the first time I noticed how weary he looked
I would rather have the oil of the sea, he said
over the grease of a KFC
give me the sound of an angry storm
over the banality of real-life TV
coffee in Styrofoam cups from faceless chains
the magazines in doctors' waiting rooms
nightclub bouncers, pencil moustaches, boy bands

cricket, government, guns,
politics, intolerance, division, war
the *Daily Mail*

he lapped at my toes in sympathy
and simply rolled away
to meet the bluey-grey of the horizon

I lay a while, then walked to a bar
and ordered a drink
I reached into my pocket to pay the barman
but all I found was a hermit crab

and I sat
and sobbed
as deep
as the ocean floor

SHADORMA INTERLUDE

bright magpie
only nonmammal
to know its
own image
one for sorrow no more, they've
discovered selfies

played *Fortnite*
non-stop for fortnight
fought eyesight
hunger thoughts
didn't eat for two weeks. can't
hold fork, knife. too weak

more tigers
in US than wild
kept as pets
caged, distressed
they long for long grass, freedom
as they're fed Frosties

he grew veg
otherworldly stuff
huge rocket
moon-size peas
onion rings of Saturn. one
giant leek for man

DUCK FEATHER

a single feather
poked through my jacket
so I pulled at it
pulled and pulled, pulled
and pulled
until out came a duck
an entire/ bemused/ duck

we stared at one another
dumbstruck

the duck was spotlessly white
as though bleached
each square inch startlingly pure
except for – a single/ brown/ hair
I paused – then I pulled there
pulled and pulled, pulled
and pulled, until lo and behold
a man emerged, six foot
head to toe, thirteen stone

he was smartly attired
sharp-suited, wine-fluted front
top label, immaculate
save for a single/ blond/ speck
on the lapel
what the heck – I pulled there
pulled and pulled, pulled
and pulled, until
with one big final pull
a woman emerged
early thirties/ professional

the man, the woman and the duck
gave one another a sideways look
then leant in towards me
and began to pluck

pulling, pulling
pulling and pulling
until finally
        out came
            this poem

A SNAIL IS JUST A SLUG ON THE PROPERTY LADDER

a snail is just a slug on the property ladder
moving smug, snug in its mobile home
every time it sees a snail, slug feels sadder
a snail is just a slug on the property ladder
open to the elements, assaulted with salt, slug gets madder
oh to have a pack on its back, be free to roam…
a snail is just a slug on the property ladder
moving smug, snug in its mobile home

FOOD PHOTOGRAPHER

photos on the menu really send you, appetise
the pictures making lies
of your lunch when it arrives
that's down to me
I'm a food click click click click photographer
I'm a yule click click click click log-rapher
I'm a hot click click click click dog-rapher
I serve up poetry in a shepherd's pie
can make a Pot Noodle smile
c'mon, sausage, give us your best side!
work it, broccoli, work it!

steaks shot at the height of their sizzle
dressings caught at the peak of their drizzle
linguini, autumn-ripe zucchini, rainbow fettuccine
quick snaps, click snaps
handy snaps of brandy snaps
candy up the menu flaps

my photos, you can taste them as I take them
smell them as I sell them
to the cookbooks and the magazines
the billboards and the TV screens
I can light a potato   just so
give it a halo, an appetising glow
I might shoot it again stood next to a drink
I might shoot it again if its eyes blink

food doesn't fidget
it has no bad side in my hands
no ego, no rueful bad profile, no entourage
no dinner sulks to be airbrushed thinner
it's just the food and the illusion of mood
oranges and limes dressed up to the nines
super-sized, caramelised, the camera lies

whatever it takes to get an image right
foam stands in   for nearly anything
polystyrene = chicken wings
and for spaghetti – string   click
and for spaghetti – string   click
and/ it's/ a/ string film   click
it's a string film   click
it's a cling film   click
it's a cling film   click
it's a wrap   click click click click

THE ISLAND OF THE SHADES

I've been to the place
where all the mislaid umbrellas and sunglasses go
to an island in the Pacific
nestled beneath a continuous rainbow
last week I journeyed there
to retrieve a favourite pair
of black shades I'd left
in a rush
on a bus

I found him there, found him happy
drinking a cocktail in a swimming pool bar
(some of the little umbrellas are gainfully employed in drinks)
he looked well, even his scratches were gone
he has many friends among the other lens
and is engaged to a parasol

we spent a few days together
in this unusual weather
I watched him revel away from the wear and tear
on our drinking binges, I saw
he was so much more
than just plastic and hinges

I came to understand this as home
a belonging I've never known
knew I'd never own him again

he asked would I like to wear him one last time
it was all I could do
to hide my eyes
the tears they cried

tears that gently pitter-pattered
on his parasol bride

HAIKU INTERLUDE II

I watch what I eat
might miss my mouth otherwise
put cake in my eye

trapped in a tower
Rapunzel lets down her hair
it holds – Tresemmé

collect Pokémon
from galaxy far away
Pikachubacca

SYLVESTER POLYESTER

ladies, put on your red shoes
you've so much to choose
      let's spend
boho beaded
mules and the wedges
rivets round the edges
      let's spend
high heels and slingbacks
and things with straps
snakeskins and moccasins
the leopard print, sequins
spend on the flip-flops
the slip-ons, the slip-offs
      let's spend
the tall boots, the thigh boots
the small boots, the high boots
the ankle boots, the calf boots
the suede boots, the half boots
      let's spend
pinky slinky espadrilles
pumps and stilettos
the open-toed sandals
the crocodile, the camel
any style, any mammal
      let's spend

ladies, you've so much to choose
ours – they come in brown or black
and they're all   called   shoes

WHITE CARRIER BAG

White Carrier Bag sits in a field
pretending to be a bird
like a pretty girl in too small a town
with one   good   gust   of wind
it might
take flight
never   to return

White Carrier Bag believes in recycling
wishes to come back as a mudguard
and tour the Ardennes
has friends in supermarkets there
how nice it would be
to be filled in on the news
rather than filled up with washing powder
food

White Carrier Bag watches a bin liner
rolling down the empty road
nice handles, it thinks to itself
and mobile…
maybe I should follow
maybe…

the sky is orange behind a scarf of low cloud
the breeze   teases

careless people never discard carrier bags –
carrier bags   escape

COMMUTING TO JUPITER

the Moon looked lonely to the girl, and shy
revealing as he did just a sliver of himself
planes and clouds drifted by with destinations in mind
stars making shows of themselves, and the Moon
the Moon looked on sadly the way a streetlight does
or a marble head
its neck too set to turn away

why don't you and the Sun hang out more?
the girl asked up at him
seems you only meet for eclipses
he's got his hat on but nowhere to go
why not take him to Aurora Borealis
catch the late show

the girl liked space – its infiniteness
the way it transported dreams

I'm going to a party and can bring a guest
come down from the heavens and accompany me
was the girl's request
there's people there would love to see you
you might meet yourself a nice little planet
and I believe there's food
Moon, you look lonely, you sure look lonely to me

the girl's mother, to her credit, took in her stride
the Moon being her daughter's chosen party guest
though she did have to put the back seats down
on her Xsara
and the Moon
the Moon felt good, to be going somewhere
he wore a tie and grinned at dogs
and cyclists and bus queues as they zipped by

at the party, streamers hung like comets from doorframes
and the way the lights were arranged over the fireplace

reminded the Moon of his friend the Plough
satellites gravitated towards the kitchen
the way satellites gravitate towards kitchens at parties
and the girl, immeasurably proud
to have the Moon as her guest, skipped on air
weightless

the other children had brought friends of their own –
the Serengeti, the Black Sea, the ozone layer
Uluru, Machu Picchu
it was a big house, you understand
though it still only had one loo

none of these guests were the Moon though
and the children flocked to him
and he carried them on his shoulders
and he illuminated the garden as evening descended
and he ate jelly
and he played musical chairs
and he laughed

on the way home the girl held his hand
and as the car turned down lit streets
their faces were ran amber black amber black
like wasps on a conveyor belt
the Moon holding with wonder, in his other hand
a party bag containing balloons
and a plastic frog
and a slice of cake
with some lettering iced in red

on her mother's steps at bedtime
the girl kissed the Moon wide of his mouth
and he blushed pink in small craters
and returned to the sky with a smile

Moon, the girl whispered
goodnight, until next fading light
she opened the door
and she stepped inside